Mysteries of the Past

A CHAPTER BOOK

By Alex Simmons

children's press®
A Division of Scholastic Inc.
New York   Toronto   London   Auckland   Sydney
Mexico City   New Delhi   Hong Kong
Danbury, Connecticut

This book is dedicated to my mother, Hortense Simmons, who taught me to face rather than flee from the unknown.

ACKNOWLEDGMENTS

The author and publisher would like to thank all those who gave their time and knowledge to help with this book. In particular, special thanks go to James P. Delgado, Executive Director, Vancouver Maritime Museum; Dennis B. Blanton, Director of the Center for Archaeological Research, College of William and Mary; Stephen B. Mabee, State Geologist/Assistant Professor, Department of Geosciences, University of Massachusetts; and Don Proulx, Professor Emeritus, Department of Anthropology, University of Massachusetts.

Library of Congress Cataloging-in-Publication Data

Simmons, Alex.
  Mysteries of the past : a chapter book / by Alex Simmons.
    p. cm. — (True tales)
  Includes bibliographical references and index.
  ISBN 0-516-25184-8 (lib. bdg.)   0-516-25451-0 (pbk.)
  1. History—Miscellanea—Juvenile literature. 2. Mary Celeste
(Brig)—Juvenile literature. 3. Roanoke Island (N. C.)—History—Juvenile literature.
4. Easter Island—Antiquities—Juvenile literature. 5. Geoglyphs—Peru—Juvenile literature.
I. Title. II. Series.
  D21.3.S48 2005
  904—dc22
                          2004028456

1 2 3 4 5 6 7 8 9 10 R 14 13 12 11 10 09 08 07 06 05

CONTENTS

INTRODUCTION

Step back in time and read about four mysteries that happened long ago.

One day in 1872, the crew and passengers aboard a ship disappeared. What happened to them? Almost three hundred years earlier, a group of English colonists vanished from an island in North Carolina. Where did they go? Giant statues dot an island in the Pacific Ocean. Why were they made? How were they moved without modern tools? In a desert in South America, large drawings cover the landscape. What was the purpose of these ancient lines?

These questions have puzzled people for hundreds of years. Will these strange cases be solved? Or will they remain mysteries forever?

CHAPTER ONE

LOST AT SEA

The *Mary Celeste* was built in 1861. For eleven years, she sailed the sea carrying **cargo** from Canada and the United States to other parts of the world. Many of those trips were filled with problems, such as fires and **collisions**. In fact, so many strange things happened that people began to wonder if the ship was **jinxed** (JINGKST).

After December 4, 1872, they were sure of it. On that day, the ship was discovered drifting in the middle of the Atlantic Ocean. Its **crew**, captain, and passengers had vanished. They were never seen again. Something had gone horribly wrong, but what?

A ship's compass

The *Mary Celeste* was a sailing ship like the
one shown above.

The ship had left New York City on November 7. It was headed for Genoa, Italy, with a cargo of 1,700 barrels of raw alcohol. The captain was Benjamin Briggs. Also on board were the captain's wife, Sarah; their two-year-old daughter, Sophia; and seven crewmen.

Twenty-seven days after the ship set sail, the crew of the Canadian ship *Dei Gratia* spotted the *Mary Celeste* drifting in the water. David Morehouse was the ship's captain and a friend of Captain Briggs. Captain Morehouse called out to the crew of the *Mary Celeste*. When no one answered, he ordered some of his men to go aboard the ship.

When the men climbed over the railing of the *Mary Celeste,* they found little damage. The sail at the front of the ship was missing, and the two hatch covers were opened. The other sails were in place, though. Two wooden **masts** stood tall and strong.

ATLANTIC OCEAN

United Kingdom

France

Portugal

Spain

MEDITERRANEAN SEA

Where the
Mary Celeste was
found drifting

Morocco

Algeria

Next, the men searched the front of the ship. They saw that the ship's only lifeboat was missing. Had the passengers and crew of the *Mary Celeste* squeezed into the tiny boat? If so, why had they abandoned the ship? There were no signs of a battle or a fire.

The men moved down the stairs. In the ship's **galley**, pots and pans were neatly arranged. The beds in the crew's cabin were made. The crew's belongings, such as books and pipes, were still there. The captain's rooms were also tidy.

The men thought there might be a clue in the captain's log. A log is a kind of notebook. Each day, the captain writes in the log about what happened on the ship. The book was no help. On a slate board, however, the men found a scribbled recording dated November 25. The note placed the *Mary Celeste* more than 300 miles (483 kilometers) from where the *Dei Gratia* found her.

An **investigation** was held in Gibraltar, an island town near Spain. The attorney general, the leader of the investigation, had many ideas as to what might have happened.

**The investigation in Gibraltar
(shown here today) lasted three months.**

His first idea was that Captain Morehouse
and his crew did away with the missing
people. He claimed that they did this in
order to get hold of the ship and her cargo.

Many people found this hard to believe.
Captain Morehouse and Captain Briggs were
known to be close friends. The two men had
even dined together the night before the
Mary Celeste set sail.

At the end of the investigation, there were still no answers. What really happened on the *Mary Celeste* remained a mystery.

A few years later, Sir Arthur Conan Doyle, the creator and writer of the *Sherlock Holmes* stories,

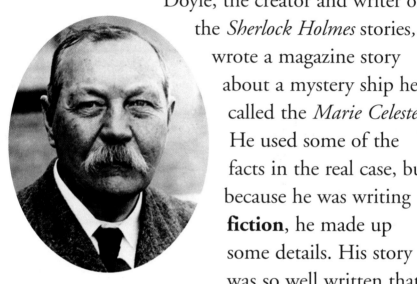

Sir Arthur Conan Doyle

wrote a magazine story about a mystery ship he called the *Marie Celeste*. He used some of the facts in the real case, but because he was writing **fiction**, he made up some details. His story was so well written that many newspaper reporters thought it was true. This made it hard for other people to investigate the real mystery. They had trouble separating the truth from Conan Doyle's fiction.

Still, even without Conan Doyle's story, the strange case of the *Mary Celeste* had enough of its own mystery to make it a **legend** forever.

CHAPTER TWO

THE MISSING COLONY

Dennis Blanton was trying to solve a mystery. About 400 years ago, a group of English settlers vanished from Roanoke Island, an island off the coast of North Carolina. Dennis was working on this missing-person case, but he is not a policeman. He is an **archaeologist** (ar-kee-OL-uh-jist). Archaeologists are like detectives. By studying objects they find, they uncover clues about the lives of people from the past.

On May 8, 1587, John White, along with 116 men, women, and children, sailed across

Dennis Blanton

Dennis went to North Carolina to
investigate a 400-year-old mystery.

A ship like the one that brought John White and other colonists to Roanoke Island

the Atlantic Ocean from England. They were headed for Chesapeake Bay, but bad weather made them stop earlier than planned. The group landed on Roanoke Island, instead. John White, as governor, guided the group as it set up the first British colony in the **New World**.

The **colonists** knew they would face many dangers. Previous colonists and soldiers had made enemies with some of the Native Americans. After many problems, the colonists had returned to England.

The people of Governor White's colony were determined to make their settlement work. They built their homes in a clearing in the woods. They hoped that one day it would become a thriving town.

Soon after the colonists landed, John White's daughter gave birth to a girl. The infant was christened Virginia Dare. Virginia became the first person to be born to English parents in the New World.

The colonists soon realized they did not have enough supplies to make it through the coming winter. Governor White arranged to sail back to England. He promised the colonists that he would return in one year. While he was away, war broke

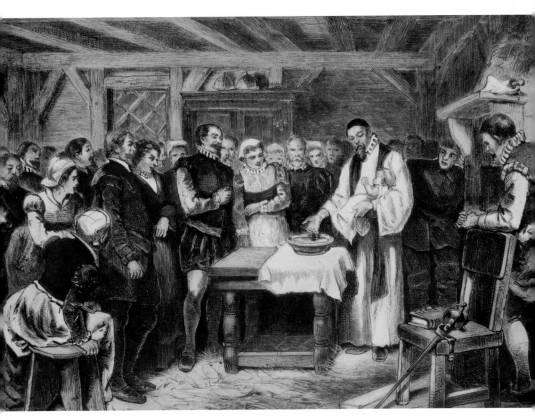

Virginia Dare was born on August 18, 1587, and baptized the following Sunday.

out between England and Spain. The war delayed his return for three years.

Governor White and his crew returned to Roanoke Island on August 17, 1590. They found the clearing deserted. Only the small houses and a wall made of standing logs remained. What had happened to the colony?

Dennis Blanton has heard many theories about the disappearances. Some people thought Native Americans had killed the colonists. Other people suspected that the colonists all died from a terrible sickness. Dennis agreed with those who believed that the colonists had moved on in search of food and supplies.

This print of a front and back view of a Native American chief is based on a drawing by John White.

This illustration shows John White discovering the tree with the mysterious word *Croatoan* carved on it.

Governor White never found signs of a battle or any graves. What he did find, though, was the word CROATOAN carved into a tree. Croatoan was the name of a nearby island. The Native Americans who lived there were friendly to the English colonists.

Governor White prepared to sail there, but a tremendous storm almost destroyed his ship. He was forced to return to England. He was never able to return to the New World to find out what had happened to his family or the other colonists.

Dennis Blanton had a plan that would help him prove his theory that the colonists had moved. He teamed up with David Stahle, a **climatologist** at the University of Arkansas. Both men knew about very old bald cypress trees growing in the swamps along the rivers that bordered Virginia and North Carolina.

As a tree grows, it adds new layers to its outer surface. Each layer covers the old one and creates a ring. One new ring is added each year. During years when a tree gets all the sun and water it needs, the layer is wider. Cypress trees can live to be over

Bald cypress trees grow in the swamplands of the Southeast.

1,000 years old, so they make excellent record keepers of an area's rainfall and snowfall.

Dennis and David found several old cypress trees. After they took samples from the core of the trees, they counted and measured the rings. The rings during the years from 1587 to 1589 were narrow and thin. This told the scientists that the

Tree rings

entire region, including Roanoke Island, had suffered a **drought** (DROUT) during that time. Very little rain fell for about three years. That meant that the colonists had been without fresh water during the time Governor White was in England. They also didn't have enough water to grow crops.

Dennis uncovered a strong reason for the colonists to leave the settlement. Still, the mystery isn't completely solved. We may never learn exactly what happened to the missing colony. Thanks to Dennis Blanton and David Stahle's research, though, we do know that John White and the other colonists settled their colony at the worst possible time.

By examining the rings of old trees, researchers solved
one part of the Roanoke mystery.

CHAPTER THREE

STONE GIANTS

Easter Island sits far out in the Pacific Ocean, about 2,300 miles (3,701 kilometers) from Chile. The people who live on this island are called the *Rapa Nui*. Their **ancestors** came here more than 800 years ago. Some people believe these ancestors traveled from a region of islands called Polynesia. Wherever they came from, they must have traveled a great distance to reach such an **isolated** place.

A stone statue on Easter Island

Easter Island is a tiny island far from any
other body of land.

For years, their **culture** grew. They built homes and boats. They caught fish and grew crops. They also did something else. They built statues. Scattered around the island are more than 800 giant statues called *moai*. They were carved out of volcanic rock between A.D. 1200 and 1600. A few are simple carvings of faces and shoulders. Others are full figures, with bodies, arms, and short legs.

No one knows why
the Rapa Nui created
such big statues. Some
scientists believe the
statues represented
their gods. Other

The moai were carved out of hardened lava.

scientists believe that the community was
divided into different groups, or clans. Each
clan built statues as **symbols** of its success. The
bigger the statue was, the greater the clan.

A line of moai face the sea.

Another mystery is how the moai were moved from the quarry to their **platforms** around the island. According to an ancient legend, the statues walked to their places of honor. This couldn't really have happened, of course. So how did the statues get to the platforms?

Patricia Vargas is the director of the Easter Island Studies Institute of Chile. She believes that the Rapa Nui used logs and rope to move the statues. This was probably the same method the Egyptians used to build the pyramids.

Patricia Vargas (standing) on Easter Island

Egyptians might have used logs to help move stones while building the pyramids.

For many years, scientists did not believe that this method could have worked on Easter Island. Moving more than eight hundred statues would require a lot of trees, and there are no trees on the island.

Then, in the early 1970s, scientists tested the island's soil and pollen and **excavated** various spots. Soon, they had gathered evidence that the landscape had once been very different. According to their findings, many types of trees grew on the island during the time the ancient Rapa Nui lived there.

Were logs from trees like this once used to move the moai?

What happened to those trees? As the Rapa Nui colony **prospered**, its population grew. In a short time, more than 8,000 people lived on the island. They built homes, farms, and storage houses for their crops. Because there are no rivers or streams on the island, the people fished in the sea. That meant they built many boats, too.

To do all this, the people would have had to cut down hundreds of trees. If they also used logs move the moai, they might have used up every tree on the small island.

In 1999, archeologist Jo Anne Van Tilburg decided to test the log-and-rope method. Jo Anne worked with a crew of sixty people. They stood two logs up and tied them behind a life-size **replica** (REP-luh-kuh) of a statue. Then they laid the

Jo Anne Van Tilburg

statue down on top of other logs that had been placed along a road. Finally, using lots of rope, they pulled the statue along until they reached their destination. It took forty people to move the statue and twenty people to stand it up. While this experiment didn't prove that this was how the moai were moved, it did prove that this method would have worked.

How and why the Rapa Nui people made these giant carvings is still a mystery. But as long as there are questions, people like Patricia Vargas and Jo Anne Van Tilburg will continue to look for answers.

CHAPTER FOUR

THE MYSTERY OF THE LINES

Jim Woodman was in a hot-air balloon. He hovered 300 feet (91 meters) over a desert in Peru. He was with Julian Nott, an **experienced** hot-air balloonist. The balloon was part of an experiment to solve an ancient puzzle.

Jim had come to Peru to study the Nazca lines. The lines are giant **geoglyphs**, or earth drawings, of animals, people, and designs. They spread out for miles in all directions. Some are over 400 feet (122 meters) long. They are so

Drawing of a geoglyph of a hummingbird

A bus drives along a road that crosses
through the Nazca lines.

huge that some can be seen in their entirety only from the air. Others can be seen at ground level, although they can best be seen by climbing the sides of hills found in the area.

The Nazca Indians created these geoglyphs between A.D. 1 and A.D. 600. They did this by brushing aside small black rocks so that the yellowish sand underneath could be seen.

The Nazca lines were discovered in the 1920s. Over the years, scientists have put forth many theories as to what the lines meant. Paul Kosok, a history professor, believed that the Nazca Indians used the lines as a guide to the movement of the stars. Other scientists wonder if they were part of an **irrigation** system. Many scientists believe they were used for religious purposes.

A geoglyph of a monkey

A writer named Erich von Daniken had an unusual theory. He claimed the lines had been used as runways for alien spaceships. He pointed out that the drawings had been made to be viewed from the sky. Therefore, they must have been meant for alien ships, since they were drawn before humans had invented airplanes or spaceships. In 1967, he wrote a book about his **theory**.

Scientists disagreed. They questioned why, if aliens had the **technology** to fly across space, they needed to draw landing patterns in the dirt.

Bill Spohrer, an American businessman living in Peru, didn't believe in aliens. However, the idea that the drawings were best viewed from the air interested him.

South America

A fire pit heats the air and causes the balloon to rise.

Bill believed that the Nazca Indians had used hot-air balloons to rise above the desert. Bill knew that huge pits had been found at the ends of many lines. In the pits were blackened rocks. Had the pits been used as launch sites for balloons?

Working with his friend, Jim Woodman, Bill made a hot-air balloon. He used only materials that the Nazca Indians might have had on hand. Cotton fabric was sewn together in the shape of an upside-down pyramid. The basket was made by weaving together long reeds. Bill and Jim called the balloon *Condor I.*

Basket of the balloon

In November 1975, the balloon was ready. Jim and his copilot, Julian Nott, soared 400 feet (122 meters) into the air. Below them were the amazing Nazca designs. After about three minutes of flight, the hot air cooled and the two men landed safely.

The experiment proved that the Nazca Indians were capable of flying in hot-air balloons. But did they? Is this why the Nazca lines were created? With no way of knowing for sure, the mystery continues.

GLOSSARY

ancestor a relative who lived long ago

archaeologist (ar-kee-OL-uh-jist) someone who studies the ancient remains of people to understand how they lived

cargo the load of goods carried by an airplane, ship, or automobile

climatologist a scientist who studies the weather and weather patterns

collision two or more things hitting each other with great force

colonist someone who lives in a newly settled place

crew a group of people who work together

culture the beliefs, practices, and arts of a group of people

drought (DROUT) a long period of dry weather

excavate to dig up something that was buried

experienced knowing a lot about a particular subject; skilled

fiction stories that tell about people and events that are not real

galley a ship's kitchen

geoglyph a drawing etched into the Earth's surface

investigation an inquiry that tries to learn the facts about something

irrigation the carrying of water to land through ditches or pipes

isolated placed apart and alone

jinx (JINGKS) to bring bad luck

legend a story, passed down through the years, that cannot be proven

mast a long pole that rises from the deck of a ship and holds the sails and ropes

New World North America and South America

platform a flat, raised structure on which something can be stood

prosper to be successful

replica (REP-luh-kuh) an exact copy of something

symbol an object or a picture that stands for something else

technology the way that people use tools, as well as the tools that they use

theory an idea that tries to explain something

FIND OUT MORE

Lost at Sea
www.maryceleste.net
Read more about the mystery ship the *Mary Celeste.*

The Missing Colony
http://www.cr.nps.gov/history/online_books/hh/16/hh16t oc.htm
Read the complete history of Roanoke Island.

Stone Giants
www.pbs.org/wgbh/nova/easter
After you explore Easter Island, find out how one team of archaeologists moved a stone statue.

The Mystery of the Lines
www.exn.ca/mysticplaces/nazcalines.asp
Find out more about the Nazca Indians and the giant line drawings they made.

More Books to Read

Easter Island: Giant Stone Statues Tell of a Rich and Tragic Past by Caroline Arnold, Houghton Mifflin, 2000

Mary Celeste: An Unsolved Mystery from History by Jane Yolen and Elizabeth Yolen-Stemple, Simon & Schuster, 2002

National Geographic Mysteries of History by Robert Stewart, National Geographic Society, 2003

Roanoke: The Lost Colony by Bob Italia, ABDO Publishing Company, 2002

INDEX

PHOTO CREDITS

MEET THE AUTHOR

 Alex Simmons has written a number of juvenile mysteries; several stage plays; three movie novelizations; and three biographies, including one on the actor Denzel Washington. Simmons also co-created an African-American hero for DC Comics. He has authored several *Scooby-Doo* comic book stories; twelve interactive mysteries for the Tiger Toys electronic game, "Who Done It;" and an acclaimed Sherlock Holmes mystery play. He is currently consulting on several exciting entertainment projects, as well as teaching two creative-arts workshops.